BAHÁ'U'LLÁH

BAHÁ'U'LLÁH

Bahái Publications Australia

Bahái Publications Australia
P.O. Box 285
Mona Vale N.S.W. 2103
Australia
Phone: 64 2 913 1554
Fax: 64 2 913 2169

ISBN 0 909991 51 0

Cover design and illustration by Peter Maguire
Glossary and Index by Barry Anderson

Typeset by Photoset Computer Service
Sydney, Australia

Printed by Ambassador Press
Sydney, Australia

Bahái International Community
Office of Public Information
New York

FOREWORD

May 29, 1992, marks the centenary of the passing of Bahá'u'lláh. His vision of humanity as one people and of the earth as a common homeland, dismissed out of hand by the world leaders to whom it was first enunciated over a hundred years ago, has today become the focus of human hope. Equally inescapable is the collapse of moral and social order, which this same declaration foresaw with awesome clarity.

The occasion has encouraged publication of this brief introduction to Bahá'u'lláh's life and work. Prepared at the request of the Universal House of Justice, trustee of the global undertaking which the events of a century ago set in motion, it offers a perspective on the feeling of confidence with which Bahá'ís the world over contemplate the future of our planet and our race.

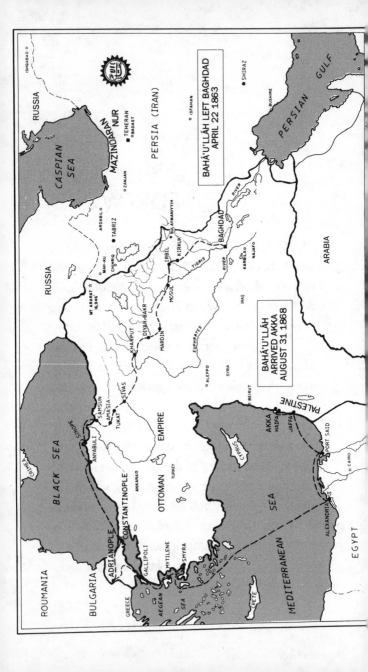

TABLE OF CONTENTS

*I*ntroduction

As the new millennium approaches, the crucial need of the human race is to find a unifying vision of the nature of man and society. For the past century humanity's response to this impulse has driven a succession of ideological upheavals that have convulsed our world and that appear now to have exhausted themselves. The passion invested in the struggle, despite its disheartening results, testifies to the depth of the need. For, without a common conviction about the course and direction of human history, it is inconceivable that foundations can be laid for a global society to which the mass of humankind can commit themselves.

Such a vision unfolds in the writings of Bahá'u'lláh, the nineteenth century prophetic figure whose growing influence is the most remarkable development of contemporary religious history. Born in Persia, November 12, 1817, Bahá'u'lláh[1] began at age 27 an undertaking that has gradually captured the imagination and loyalty of several million people from virtually every race, culture, class, and nation on earth. The phenomenon is one that has no reference points in the contemporary world, but is associated rather with climactic changes of

1

direction in the collective past of the human race. For Bahá'u'lláh claimed to be no less than the Messenger of God to the age of human maturity, the Bearer of a Divine Revelation that fulfills the promises made in earlier religions, and that will generate the spiritual nerves and sinews for the unification of the peoples of the world. ⌐

If they were to do nothing else, the effects which Bahá'u'lláh's life and writings have already had should command the earnest attention of anyone who believes that human nature is fundamentally spiritual and that the coming organization of our planet must be informed by this aspect of reality. The documentation lies open to general scrutiny. For the first time in history humanity has available a detailed and verifiable record of the birth of an independent religious system and of the life of its Founder. Equally accessible is the record of the response that the new faith has evoked, through the emergence of a global community which can already justly claim to represent a microcosm of the human race.[2]

During the earlier decades of this century, this development was relatively obscure. Bahá'u'lláh's writings forbid the aggressive proselytism through which many religious messages have been widely promulgated. Further, the priority which the Bahá'í community gave to the establishment of groups at the local level throughout the entire planet militated against the early emergence of large concentrations of adherents in any one country or the mobilization of resources required for large-scale programs of public information. Arnold Toynbee, intrigued by phenomena that might represent the emergence of a new universal religion, noted in the 1950s that the Bahá'í Faith was then about as familiar to the average educated Westerner as Christianity had been to the corresponding class in the Roman empire during the second century A.D.[3]

In more recent years, as the Bahá'í community's numbers have rapidly increased in many countries, the situation has changed dramatically. There is now virtually no area in the world where the pattern of life taught by Bahá'u'lláh is not taking root. The respect which the community's social and economic development projects are beginning to win in governmental, academic, and United Nations circles further reinforces the argument for a detached and serious examination of the impulse behind a process of social transformation that is, in critical respects, unique in our world.

No uncertainty surrounds the nature of the generating impulse. Bahá'u'lláh's writings cover an enormous range of subjects from social issues such as racial integration, the equality of the sexes, and disarmament, to those questions that affect the innermost life of the human soul. The original texts, many of them in His own hand, the others dictated and affirmed by their author, have been meticulously preserved. For several decades, a systematic program of translation and publication has made selections from Bahá'u'lláh's writings accessible to people everywhere, in over eight hundred languages.

*B*irth of a New Revelation

Bahá'u'lláh's mission began in a subterranean dungeon in Teheran in August 1852. Born into a noble family that could trace its ancestry back to the great dynasties of Persia's imperial past, He declined the ministerial career open to Him in government, and chose instead to devote His energies to a range of philanthropies which had, by the early 1840s, earned Him widespread renown as "Father of the Poor." This privileged existence swiftly eroded after 1844, when Bahá'u'lláh became one of the leading advocates of a movement that was to change the course of His country's history.

The early nineteenth century was a period of messianic expectations in many lands. Deeply disturbed by the implications of scientific inquiry and industrialization, earnest believers from many religious backgrounds turned to the scriptures of their faiths for an understanding of the accelerating processes of change. In Europe and America groups like the Templers and the Millerites believed they had found in the Christian scriptures evidence supporting their conviction that history had ended and the return of Jesus Christ was at hand. A markedly similar ferment developed in the Middle East around the belief that the fulfillment of various prophecies in the Qur'án and Islamic Traditions was imminent.

By far the most dramatic of these millennialist movements had been the one in Persia, which had focused on the person and teachings of a young merchant from the city of Shiraz, known to history as the Báb.[4] For nine

4

years, from 1844 to 1853, Persians of all classes had been caught up in a storm of hope and excitement aroused by the Báb's announcement that the Day of God was at hand and that He was himself the One promised in Islamic scripture. Humanity stood, He said, on the threshold of an era that would witness the restructuring of all aspects of life. New fields of learning, as yet inconceivable, would permit even the children of the new age to surpass the most erudite of contemporary scholars. The human race was called by God to embrace these changes through undertaking a transformation of its moral and spiritual life. His own mission was to prepare humanity for the event that lay at the heart of these developments, the coming of that universal Messenger of God, "*He Whom God will make manifest*," awaited by the followers of all religions.[5]

The claim had evoked violent hostility from the Muslim clergy, who taught that the process of Divine Revelation had ended with Muhammad, and that any assertion to the contrary represented apostasy, punishable by death. Their denunciation of the Báb had soon enlisted the support of the Persian authorities. Thousands of followers of the new faith had perished in a horrific series of massacres throughout the country, and the Báb had been publicly executed on July 9, 1850.[6] In an age of growing Western involvement in the Orient, these events aroused interest and compassion in influential European circles. The nobility of the Báb's life and teachings, the heroism of His followers, and the hope for fundamental reform that they had kindled in a darkened land had exerted a powerful attraction for personalities ranging from Ernest Renan and Leo Tolstoy to Sarah Bernhardt and the Comte de Gobineau.[7]

Because of His prominence in the defense of the Báb's cause, Bahá'u'lláh was arrested and brought, in chains and on foot, to Teheran. Protected in some measure by an impressive personal reputation and the social position of His family, as well as by protests which the Bábí pogroms had evoked from Western embassies, He was not sentenced to death, as influential figures at the royal court were urging. Instead, He was cast into the notorious Síyáh-Chál, the "Black Pit," a deep, vermin-infested dungeon which had been created in one of the city's abandoned reservoirs. No charges were laid but He and some thirty companions were, without appeal, kept immured in the darkness and filth of this pit, surrounded by hardened criminals, many of them under sentence of death. Around Bahá'u'lláh's neck was clamped a heavy chain, so notorious in penal circles as to have been given its own name. When He did not quickly perish, as had been expected, an attempt was made to poison Him. The marks of the chain were to remain on His body for the rest of His life.

Central to Bahá'u'lláh's writings is an exposition of the great themes which have preoccupied religious thinkers throughout the ages: God, the role of Revelation in history, the relationship of the world's religious systems to one another, the meaning of faith, and the basis of moral authority in the organization of human society. Passages in these texts speak intimately of His own spiritual experience, of His response to the Divine summons, and of the dialogue with the "Spirit of God" which lay at the heart of His mission. Religious history has never before offered the inquirer the opportunity for so candid an encounter with the phenomenon of Divine Revelation.

Toward the end of His life, Bahá'u'lláh's writings on His early experiences included a brief description of the conditions in the Síyáh-Chál:

We were consigned for four months to a place foul beyond comparison.... The dungeon was wrapped in thick darkness, and Our fellow-prisoners numbered nearly a hundred and fifty souls: thieves, assassins and highwaymen. Though crowded, it had no other outlet than the passage by which We entered. No pen can depict that place, nor any tongue describe its loathsome smell. Most of these men had neither clothes nor bedding to lie on. God alone knoweth what befell Us in that most foul-smelling and gloomy place![8]

Each day the guards would descend the three steep flights of stairs of the pit, seize one or more of the prisoners, and drag them out to be executed. In the streets of Teheran, Western observers were appalled by scenes of Bábí victims blown from cannon mouths, hacked to death by axes and swords, and led to their deaths with burning candles inserted into open wounds in their bodies.[9] It was in these circumstances, and faced with the prospect of His own imminent death, that Bahá'u'lláh received the first intimation of His mission:

One night, in a dream these exalted words were heard on every side: "Verily, We shall render Thee victorious by Thyself and by Thy Pen. Grieve Thou not for that which hath befallen Thee, neither be Thou afraid, for Thou art in safety. Erelong will God raise up the treasures of the earth — men who will aid Thee through Thyself and through Thy name, wherewith God hath revived the hearts of such as have recognized Him.[10]

The experience of Divine Revelation, touched on only at secondhand in surviving accounts of the lives of the Buddha, Moses, Jesus Christ, and Muḥammad, is described graphically in Bahá'u'lláh's own words:

During the days I lay in the prison of Ṭihrán, though the galling weight of the chains and the stench-filled air allowed Me but little sleep, still in those infrequent moments of slumber I felt as if something flowed from the crown of My head over My breast, even as a mighty torrent that precipitateth itself upon the earth from the summit of a lofty mountain. Every limb of My body would, as a result, be set afire. At such moments My tongue recited what no man could bear to hear.[11]

*E*xile

Eventually, still without trial or recourse, Bahá'u'lláh was released from prison and immediately banished from His native land, His wealth and properties arbitrarily confiscated. The Russian diplomatic representative, who knew Him personally and who had followed the Bábí persecutions with growing distress, offered Him his protection and refuge in lands under the control of his government. In the prevailing political climate, acceptance of such help would almost certainly have been misrepresented by others as having political implications.[12] Perhaps for this reason, Bahá'u'lláh chose to accept banishment to the neighboring territory of Iraq, then under the rule of the Ottoman Empire. This expulsion was the beginning of forty years of exile, imprisonment, and bitter persecution.

In the years which immediately followed His departure from Persia, Bahá'u'lláh gave priority to the needs of the Bábí community which had gathered in Baghdad, a task which had devolved on Him as the only effective Bábí leader to have survived the massacres. The death of the Báb and the almost simultaneous loss of most of the young faith's teachers and guides had left the body of the believers scattered and demoralized. When His efforts to rally those who had fled to Iraq aroused jealousy and dissension,[13] He followed the path that had been taken by all of the Messengers of God gone before Him, and withdrew to the wilderness, choosing for the purpose the mountain region of Kurdistan. His withdrawal, as He later said, had

9

"contemplated no return." Its reason "was to avoid becoming a subject of discord among the faithful, a source of disturbance unto Our companions." Although the two years spent in Kurdistan were a period of intense privation and physical hardship, Bahá'u'lláh describes them as a time of profound happiness during which He reflected deeply on the message entrusted to Him: "*Alone, We communed with Our spirit, oblivious of the world and all that is therein.*"[14]

Only with great reluctance, believing it His responsibility to the cause of the Báb, did He eventually accede to urgent messages from the remnant of the desperate group of exiles in Baghdad who had discovered His whereabouts and appealed to Him to return and assume the leadership of their community.

Two of the most important volumes of Bahá'u'lláh's writings date from this first period of exile, preceding the declaration of His mission in 1863. The first of these is a small book which He named *The Hidden Words*. Written in the form of a compilation of moral aphorisms, the volume represents the ethical heart of Bahá'u'lláh's message. In verses which Bahá'u'lláh describes as a distillation of the spiritual guidance of all the Revelations of the past, the voice of God speaks directly to the human soul:

O Son of Spirit!

The best beloved of all things in My sight is Justice; turn not away therefrom if thou desirest Me, and neglect it not that I may confide in thee. By its aid thou shalt see with thine own eyes and not through the eyes of others, and shalt know of thine own knowledge and not through the knowledge of thy neighbor. Ponder this in thy heart; how it behooveth thee to be. Verily justice is My gift to thee and the sign of My loving-kindness. Set it then before thine eyes.

O Son of Being!

Love Me that I may love thee. If thou lovest Me not, My love can in no wise reach thee. Know this, O servant.

O Son of Man!

Sorrow not save that thou art far from Us. Rejoice not save that thou art drawing near and returning unto Us....

O Son of Being!

With the hands of power I made thee and with the fingers of strength I created thee; and within thee have I placed the essence of My light. Be thou content with it and seek naught else, for My work is perfect and My command is binding. Question it not, nor have a doubt thereof.[15]

The second of the two major works composed by Bahá'u'lláh during this period is *The Book of Certitude*, a comprehensive exposition of the nature and purpose of religion. In passages that draw not only on the Qur'án, but with equal facility and insight on the Old and New Testaments, the Messengers of God are depicted as agents of a single, unbroken process, the awakening of the human race to its spiritual and moral potentialities. A humanity which has come of age can respond to a directness of teaching that goes beyond the language of parable and allegory; faith is a matter not of blind belief, but of conscious knowledge. Nor is the guidance of an ecclesiastical elite any longer required: the gift of reason confers on each individual in this new age of enlightenment and education the capacity to respond to Divine guidance. The test is that of sincerity:

> No man shall attain the shores of the ocean of true understanding except he be detached from all that is in heaven and on earth.... The essence of these words is this: they that tread the path of faith, they that thirst for the wine of certitude, must cleanse themselves of all that is earthly – their ears from idle talk, their minds from vain imaginings, their hearts from worldly affections, their eyes from that which perisheth. They should put their trust in God, and, holding fast unto Him, follow in His way. Then will they be made worthy of the effulgent glories of the sun of divine knowledge and understanding, ... inasmuch as man can never hope to attain unto the knowledge of the All-Glorious ... unless and until he ceases to regard the words and deeds of mortal men as a standard for the true understanding and recognition of God and His Prophets.

> Consider the past. How many, both high and low, have, at all times, yearningly awaited the advent of the Manifestations of God in the sanctified persons of His chosen Ones.... And whensoever the portals of grace did open, and the clouds of divine bounty did rain upon mankind, and the light of the Unseen did shine above the horizon of celestial might, they all denied Him, and turned away from His face – the face of God Himself....

> Only when the lamp of search, of earnest striving, of longing desire, of passionate devotion, of fervid love, of rapture, and ecstasy, is kindled within the seeker's heart, and the breeze of His loving-kindness is wafted upon his soul, will the darkness of error be dispelled, the mists of doubts and misgivings be dissipated,

*and the lights of knowledge and certitude
envelop his being.... Then will the manifold
favors and outpouring grace of the holy and
everlasting Spirit confer such new life upon the
seeker that he will find himself endowed with a
new eye, a new ear, a new heart, and a new
mind.... Gazing with the eye of God, he will
perceive within every atom a door that leadeth
him to the stations of absolute certitude. He will
discover in all things the ... evidences of an
everlasting Manifestation.*

*... When the channel of the human soul is
cleansed of all worldly and impeding
attachments, it will unfailingly perceive the
breath of the Beloved across immeasurable
distances, and will, led by its perfume, attain
and enter the City of Certitude....*

*... That city is none other than the Word of God
revealed in every age and dispensation.... All
the guidance, the blessings, the learning, the
understanding, the faith, and certitude,
conferred upon all that is in heaven and on
earth, are hidden and treasured within these
Cities.*[16]

No overt reference is made to
Bahá'u'lláh's own as yet unannounced mission;
rather, *The Book of Certitude* is organized around
a vigorous exposition of the mission of the
martyred Báb. Not the least of the reasons for the
book's powerful influence on the Bábí
community, which included a number of scholars
and former seminarians, was the mastery of
Islamic thought and teaching its author displays in
demonstrating the Báb's claim to have fulfilled the
prophecies of Islam. Calling on the Bábís to be
worthy of the trust which the Báb had placed in
them and of the sacrifice of so many heroic lives,
Bahá'u'lláh held out before them the challenge

not only of bringing their personal lives into conformity with the Divine teachings, but of making their community a model for the heterogeneous population of Baghdad, the Iraqi provincial capital.

Though living in very straitened material circumstances, the exiles were galvanized by this vision. One of their company, a man called Nabíl, who was later to leave a detailed history of both the ministries of the Báb and Bahá'u'lláh, has described the spiritual intensity of those days:

> Many a night no less than ten persons subsisted on no more than a pennyworth of dates. No one knew to whom actually belonged the shoes, the cloaks, or the robes that were to be found in their houses. Whoever went to the bazaar could claim that the shoes upon his feet were his own, and each one who entered the presence of Bahá'u'lláh could affirm that the cloak and robe he then wore belonged to him.... O, for the joy of those days, and the gladness and wonder of those hours![17]

To the dismay of the Persian consular authorities who had believed the Bábí "episode" to have run its course, the community of exiles gradually became a respected and influential element in Iraq's provincial capital and the neighboring towns. Since several of the most important shrines of Shi'ih Islam were located in the area, a steady stream of Persian pilgrims was also exposed, under the most favorable circumstances, to the renewal of Bábí influence. Among dignitaries who called on Bahá'u'lláh in the simple house He occupied were princes of the royal family. So enchanted by the experience was one of them that he conceived the somewhat naive idea that by erecting a duplicate of the building in the gardens of his own estate, he might recapture something of the atmosphere of spiritual purity and detachment he had briefly encountered. Another, more deeply moved by the experience of his visit, expressed to friends the feeling that "were all the sorrows of the world to be crowded into my heart they would, I feel, all vanish, when in the presence of Bahá'u'lláh. It is as if I had entered Paradise..."[18]

The Declaration in the Riḍván Garden

By 1863, Bahá'u'lláh concluded that the time had come to begin acquainting some of those around Him with the mission which had been entrusted to Him in the darkness of the Síyáh-Chál.

This decision coincided with a new stage in the campaign of opposition to His work, which had been relentlessly pursued by the Shi'ih Muslim clergy and representatives of the Persian government. Fearing that the acclaim which Bahá'u'lláh was beginning to enjoy among influential Persian visitors to Iraq would re-ignite popular enthusiasm in Persia, the Shah's government pressed the Ottoman authorities to remove Him far from the borders and into the interior of the empire. Eventually, the Turkish government acceded to these pressures and invited the exile, as its guest, to make His residence in the capital, Constantinople. Despite the courteous terms in which the message was couched, the intention was clearly to require compliance.[19]

By this time, the devotion of the little company of exiles had come to focus on Bahá'u'lláh's person as well as on His exposition of the Báb's teachings. A growing number of them had become convinced that He was speaking not only as the Báb's advocate, but on behalf of the far greater cause which the latter had declared to be imminent. These beliefs became a certainty in late April 1863 when Bahá'u'lláh, on the eve of His departure for Constantinople, called together individuals among His companions, in a garden to which was later given the name Riḍván ("Paradise"), and confided the central fact of His mission. Over the next four years, although no open announcement was considered timely, the hearers gradually shared with trusted friends the news that the Báb's promises had been fulfilled and that the "Day of God" had dawned.

The precise circumstances surrounding this private communication are, in the words of the Bahá'í authority most intimately familiar with the records of the period, "shrouded in an obscurity which future historians will find it difficult to penetrate."[20] The nature of the declaration may be appreciated in various references which Bahá'u'lláh was to make to His mission in many of His subsequent writings:

> The purpose underlying all creation is the revelation of this most sublime, this most holy Day, the Day known as the Day of God, in His Books and Scriptures – the Day which all the Prophets, and the Chosen Ones, and the holy ones, have wished to witness.[21]

> ...this is the Day in which mankind can behold the Face, and hear the Voice, of the Promised One. The Call of God hath been raised, and the light of His countenance hath been lifted up upon men. It behooveth every man to blot out the trace of every idle word from the tablet of his heart, and to gaze, with an open and unbiased mind, on the signs of His Revelation, the proofs of His Mission, and the tokens of His glory.[22]

As repeatedly emphasized in Bahá'u'lláh's exposition of the Báb's message, the primary purpose of God in revealing His Will is to effect a transformation in the character of humankind, to

17

develop within those who respond, the moral and spiritual qualities that are latent within human nature:

Beautify your tongues, O people with truthfulness, and adorn your souls with the ornament of honesty. Beware, O people, that ye deal not treacherously with any one. Be ye the trustees of God amongst His creatures, and emblems of His generosity amidst His people....[23]

Illumine and hallow your hearts; let them not be profaned by the thorns of hate or the thistles of malice. Ye dwell in one world, and have been created through the operation of one Will. Blessed is he who mingleth with all men in a spirit of utmost kindliness and love.[24]

The aggressive proselytism that had characterized efforts in ages past to promote the cause of religion is declared to be unworthy of the Day of God. Each person who has recognized the Revelation has the obligation to share it with those who he believes are seeking, but to leave the response entirely to his hearers:

Show forbearance and benevolence and love to one another. Should any one among you be incapable of grasping a certain truth, or be striving to comprehend it, show forth, when conversing with him, a spirit of extreme kindliness and good-will....[25]

The whole duty of man in this Day is to attain that share of the flood of grace which God poureth forth for him. Let none, therefore, consider the largeness or smallness of the receptacle....[26]

Against the background of the bloody events in Persia, Bahá'u'lláh not only told His followers that "*if ye be slain, it is better for you than to slay,*" but urged them to set an example of obedience to civil authority: "*In every country where any of this people reside, they must behave towards the government of that country with loyalty, honesty and truthfulness.*"[27]

The conditions surrounding Bahá'u'lláh's departure from Baghdad provided a dramatic demonstration of the potency of these principles. In only a few years, a band of foreign exiles whose arrival in the area had aroused suspicion and aversion on the part of their neighbors had become one of the most respected and influential segments of the population. They supported themselves through flourishing businesses; as a group they were admired for their generosity and the integrity of their conduct; the lurid allegations of religious fanaticism and violence, sedulously spread by Persian consular officials and members of the Shi'ih Muslim clergy, had ceased to have an effect on the public mind. By May 3, 1863, when He rode out of Baghdad, accompanied by His family and those of His companions and servants who had been chosen to accompany Him to Constantinople, Bahá'u'lláh had become an immensely popular and cherished figure. In the days immediately preceding the leave-taking a stream of notables, including the governor of the province himself, came to the garden where He had temporarily taken up residence, many of them from great distances, in order to pay their respects. Eyewitnesses to the departure have described in moving terms the acclaim that greeted Him, the tears of many of the onlookers, and the concern of the Ottoman authorities and civil officials to do their visitor honor.[28]

"*The* Changeless Faith of God..."

Following the declaration of His mission in 1863, Bahá'u'lláh began to elaborate a theme already introduced in *The Book of Certitude*, the relationship between the Will of God and the evolutionary process by which the spiritual and moral capacities latent in human nature find expression. This exposition would occupy a central place in His writings over the remaining thirty years of His life. The reality of God, He asserts, is and will always remain unknowable. Whatever words human thought may apply to the Divine nature relate only to human existence and are the products of human efforts to describe human experience:

> *Far, far from Thy glory be what mortal man can affirm of Thee, or attribute unto Thee, or the praise with which he can glorify Thee! Whatever duty Thou hast prescribed unto Thy servants of extolling to the utmost Thy majesty and glory is but a token of Thy grace unto them, that they may be enabled to ascend unto the station conferred upon their own inmost being, the station of the knowledge of their own selves.* [29]

> *To every discerning and illumined heart it is evident that God, the unknowable Essence, the divine Being, is immensely exalted beyond every human attribute, such as corporeal existence, ascent and descent, egress and regress. Far be it from His glory that human tongue should adequately recount His praise, or that human heart comprehend His fathomless mystery. He is and hath ever been veiled in the ancient eternity*

of His Essence, and will remain in His Reality everlastingly hidden from the sight of men....[30]

What humanity experiences in turning to the Creator of all existence are the attributes or qualities which are associated with God's recurring Revelations:

> The door of the knowledge of the Ancient of Days being thus closed in the face of all beings, the Source of infinite grace, ... hath caused those luminous Gems of Holiness to appear out of the realm of the spirit, in the noble form of the human temple, and be made manifest unto all men, that they may impart unto the world the mysteries of the unchangeable Being, and tell of the subtleties of His imperishable Essence....[31]

> These sanctified Mirrors ... are one and all the Exponents on earth of Him Who is the central Orb of the universe, its Essence and ultimate Purpose. From Him proceed their knowledge and power; from Him is derived their sovereignty. The beauty of their countenance is but a reflection of His image, and their revelation a sign of His deathless glory....[32]

The Revelations of God do not differ in any essential respect from one another, although the changing needs they serve from age to age have called out unique responses from each of them:

> These attributes of God are not and have never been vouchsafed specially unto certain Prophets, and withheld from others. Nay, all the Prophets of God, His well-favored, His holy, and chosen Messengers, are, without exception, the bearers of His names, and the embodiments of His attributes. They only differ in the intensity of their revelation, and the comparative potency of their light....[33]

Students of religion are cautioned not to permit theological dogmas or other preconceptions to lead them into discriminating among those whom God has used as channels of His light:

Beware, O believers in the Unity of God, lest ye be tempted to make any distinction between any of the Manifestations of His Cause, or to discriminate against the signs that have accompanied and proclaimed their Revelation. This indeed is the true meaning of Divine Unity, if ye be of them that apprehend and believe this truth. Be ye assured, moreover, that the works and acts of each and every one of these Manifestations of God, nay whatever pertaineth unto them, and whatsoever they may manifest in the future, are all ordained by God, and are a reflection of His Will and Purpose.... [34]

Bahá'u'lláh compares the interventions of the Divine Revelations to the return of spring. The Messengers of God are not merely teachers, although this is one of their primary functions. Rather, the spirit of their words, together with the example of their lives, has the capacity to tap the roots of human motivation and to induce fundamental and lasting change. Their influence opens new realms of understanding and achievement:

And since there can be no tie of direct intercourse to bind the one true God with His creation, and no resemblance whatever can exist between the transient and the Eternal, the contingent and the Absolute, He hath ordained that in every age and dispensation a pure and stainless Soul be made manifest in the kingdoms of earth and heaven.... Led by the light of unfailing guidance, and invested with supreme sovereignty, They [the Messengers of God] are commissioned to use the inspiration of Their words, the effusions of Their infallible grace and the sanctifying breeze of Their Revelation for the cleansing of every longing heart and receptive spirit from the dross and dust of earthly cares and limitations. Then, and only then, will the Trust of God, latent in the reality of man, emerge ... and implant the ensign of its revealed glory upon the summits of men's hearts.[35]

Without this intervention from the world of God, human nature remains the captive of instinct, as well as of unconscious assumptions and patterns of behavior that have been culturally determined:

Having created the world and all that liveth and moveth therein, He [God] ... chose to confer upon man the unique distinction and capacity to know Him and to love Him – a capacity that must needs be regarded as the generating impulse and the primary purpose underlying the whole of creation.... Upon the inmost reality of each and every created thing He hath shed the light of one of His names, and made it a recipient of the glory of one of His attributes. Upon the reality of man, however, He hath focused the radiance of all of His names and attributes, and made it a mirror of His own Self. Alone of all created things man hath been singled out for so great a favor, so enduring a bounty.

These energies with which the ... Source of heavenly guidance hath endowed the reality of man lie, however, latent within him, even as the flame is hidden within the candle and the rays of light are potentially present in the lamp. The radiance of these energies may be obscured by worldly desires even as the light of the sun can be concealed beneath the dust and dross which cover the mirror. Neither the candle nor the lamp can be lighted through their own unaided efforts, nor can it ever be possible for the mirror to free itself from its dross. It is clear and evident that until a fire is kindled the lamp will never be ignited, and unless the dross is blotted out from the face of the mirror it can never represent the image of the sun nor reflect its light and glory.[36]

The time has come, Bahá'u'lláh said, when humanity has both the capacity and the opportunity to see the entire panorama of its spiritual development as a single process: *"Peerless is this Day, for it is as the eye to past ages and centuries, and as a light unto the darkness of the times."*[37] In this perspective, the followers of differing religious traditions must strive to understand what He called *"the changeless Faith of God"*[38] and to distinguish its central spiritual impulse from the changing laws and concepts that were revealed to meet the requirements of an ever-evolving human society:

The Prophets of God should be regarded as physicians whose task is to foster the well-being of the world and its peoples, that, through the spirit of oneness, they may heal the sickness of a divided humanity.... Little wonder, then, if the treatment prescribed by the physician in this day should not be found to be identical with that which he prescribed before. How could it be otherwise when the ills affecting the sufferer necessitate at every stage of his sickness a special remedy? In like manner, every time the Prophets of God have illumined the world with the resplendent radiance of the Day Star of Divine knowledge, they have invariably summoned its peoples to embrace the light of God through such means as best befitted the

24

exigencies of the age in which they appeared....[39]

It is not only the heart, but the mind, which must devote itself to this process of discovery. Reason, Bahá'u'lláh asserts, is God's greatest gift to the soul, "*a sign of the revelation of ... the sovereign Lord.*"[40] Only by freeing itself from inherited dogma, whether religious or materialistic, can the mind take up an independent exploration of the relationship between the Word of God and the experience of humankind. In such a search, a major obstacle is prejudice: "*Warn ... the beloved of the one true God, not to view with too critical an eye the sayings and writings of men. Let them rather approach such sayings and writings in a spirit of open-mindedness and loving sympathy.*"[41]

*T*he Manifestation of God

What is common to all who are devoted to one or another of the world's religious systems is the conviction that it is through the Divine Revelation that the soul comes in touch with the world of God, and that it is this relationship which gives real meaning to life. Some of the most important passages in Bahá'u'lláh's writings are those which discuss at length the nature and role of those who are the channels of this Revelation, the Messengers or "Manifestations of God." A recurrent analogy found in these passages is that of the physical sun. While the latter shares certain characteristics of the other bodies in the solar system, it differs from them in that it is, in itself, the source of the system's light. The planets and moons reflect light whereas the sun emits it as an attribute inseparable from its nature. The system revolves around this focal point, each of its members influenced not only by its particular composition, but by its relationship to the source of the system's light.[42]

In the same way, Bahá'u'lláh asserts, the human personality which the Manifestation of God shares with the rest of the race is differentiated from others in a way that fits it to serve as the channel or vehicle for the Revelation of God. Apparently contradictory references to this dual station, attributed, for example, to Christ,[43] have been among the many sources of religious confusion and dissension throughout history. Bahá'u'lláh says on the subject:

Whatever is in the heavens and whatever is on the earth is a direct evidence of the revelation

*within it of the attributes and names of God ...
To a supreme degree is this true of man, who,
among all created things, ... hath been singled
out for the glory of such distinction. For in him are
potentially revealed all the attributes and names
of God to a degree that no other created being
hath excelled or surpassed.... And of all men,
the most accomplished, the most distinguished,
and the most excellent are the Manifestations of
the Sun of Truth. Nay, all else besides these
Manifestations, live by the operation of their
Will, and move and have their being through
the outpourings of their grace.*[44]

Throughout history, the conviction of
believers that the Founder of their own religion
occupied a unique station has had the effect of
stimulating intense speculation on the nature of
the Manifestation of God. Such speculation has,
however, been, severely hampered by the
difficulties of interpreting and resolving the
allegorical allusions in past scriptures. The attempt
to crystallize opinion in the form of religious
dogma has been a divisive rather than unifying
force in history. Indeed, despite the enormous
energy devoted to theological pursuits – or
perhaps because of it – today there are profound
differences among Muslims as to the precise
station of Muḥammad, among Christians as to that
of Jesus, and among Buddhists with respect to the
Founder of their own religion. As is all too
apparent, the controversies created by these and
other differences within any one given tradition
have proven at least as acute as those separating
that tradition from its sister faiths.

Particularly important to an understanding
of Bahá'u'lláh's teachings on the unity of
religions, therefore, are His statements about the
station of the successive Messengers of God and

the functions performed by them in the spiritual history of humankind:

[The] Manifestations of God have each a twofold station. One is the station of pure abstraction and essential unity. In this respect, if thou callest them all by one name, and dost ascribe to them the same attributes, thou hast not erred from the truth....

The other station is the station of distinction, and pertaineth to the world of creation, and to the limitations thereof. In this respect, each Manifestation of God hath a distinct individuality, a definitely prescribed mission, a predestined revelation, and specially designated limitations. Each one of them is known by a different name, is characterized by a special attribute, fulfills a definite mission...

Viewed in the light of their second station ... they manifest absolute servitude, utter destitution, and complete self-effacement. Even as He saith: "I am the servant of God. I am but a man like you." ...

Were any of the all-embracing Manifestations of God to declare: "I am God," He, verily, speaketh the truth, and no doubt attacheth thereto. For ... through their Revelation, their attributes and names, the Revelation of God, His names and His attributes, are made manifest in the world.... And were any of them to voice the utterance, "I am the Messenger of God," He, also, speaketh the truth, the indubitable truth.... Viewed in this light, they are all but Messengers of that ideal King, that unchangeable Essence.... And were they to say, "We are the Servants of God," this also is a manifest and indisputable fact. For they have been made manifest in the uttermost state of servitude, a servitude the like of which no man can possibly attain....[45]

Thus it is that whatsoever be their utterance, whether it pertain to the realm of Divinity, Lordship, Prophethood, Messengership, Guardianship, Apostleship, or Servitude, all is true, beyond the shadow of a doubt. Therefore these sayings ... must be attentively considered, that the divergent utterances of the Manifestations of the Unseen and Day Springs of Holiness may cease to agitate the soul and perplex the mind.[46]

"*An* Ever-Advancing Civilization..."

Implicit in these paragraphs is a perspective which represents the most challenging feature of Bahá'u'lláh's exposition of the function of the Manifestation of God. Divine Revelation is, He says, the motive power of civilization. When it occurs, its transforming effect on the minds and souls of those who respond to it is replicated in the new society that slowly takes shape around their experience. A new center of loyalty emerges that can win the commitment of peoples from the widest range of cultures; music and the arts seize on symbols that mediate far richer and more mature inspirations; a radical redefinition of concepts of right and wrong makes possible the formulation of new codes of civil law and conduct; new institutions are conceived in order to give expression to impulses of moral responsibility previously ignored or unknown: "He was in the world, and the world was made by him..."[47] As the new culture evolves into a civilization, it assimilates achievements and insights of past eras in a multitude of fresh permutations. Features of past cultures that cannot by incorporated atrophy or are taken up by marginal elements among the population. The Word of God creates new possibilities within both the individual consciousness and human relationships.

Every word that proceedeth out of the mouth of God is endowed with such potency as can instill new life into every human frame ... All the wondrous works ye behold in this world have been manifested through the operation of His supreme and most exalted Will, His wondrous and inflexible Purpose ... No sooner is this resplendent word uttered, than its animating energies, stirring within all created things, give birth to the means and instruments whereby such arts can be produced and perfected ... In the days to come, ye will, verily, behold things of which ye have never heard before ... Every single letter proceeding out of the mouth of God is indeed a mother letter, and every word uttered by Him Who is the Well Spring of Divine Revelation is a mother word ...[48]

The sequence of the Divine Revelations, Bahá'u'lláh asserts, is "*a process that hath had no beginning and will have no end.*"[49] Although the mission of each of the Manifestations is limited in time and in the functions it performs, it is an integral part of an ongoing and progressive unfoldment of God's power and will:

Contemplate with thine inward eye the chain of successive Revelations that hath linked the Manifestation of Adam with that of the Báb. I testify before God that each one of these Manifestations hath been sent down through the operation of the Divine Will and Purpose, that each hath been the bearer of a specific Message, that each hath been entrusted with a divinely revealed Book ... The measure of the Revelation with which every one of them hath been identified had been definitely foreordained ...[50]

Eventually, as an ever-evolving civilization exhausts its spiritual sources, a process of disintegration sets in, as it does throughout the phenomenal world. Turning again to analogies offered by nature, Bahá'u'lláh compares this hiatus in the development of civilization to the onset of winter. Moral vitality diminishes, as does social cohesion. Challenges which would have been overcome at an earlier age, or been turned into opportunities for exploration and achievement, become insuperable barriers. Religion loses its relevance, and experimentation becomes increasingly fragmented, further deepening social divisions. Increasingly, uncertainty about the meaning and value of life generates anxiety and confusion. Speaking about this condition in our own age Bahá'u'lláh says:

We can well perceive how the whole human race is encompassed with great, with incalculable afflictions. We see it languishing on its bed of sickness, sore-tried and disillusioned. They that are intoxicated by self-conceit have interposed themselves between it and the Divine and infallible Physician. Witness how they have entangled all men, themselves included, in the mesh of their devices. They can neither discover the cause of the disease, nor have they any knowledge of the remedy. They have conceived the straight to be crooked, and have imagined their friend an enemy.[51]

When each of the Divine impulses has fulfilled itself, the process recurs. A new Manifestation of God appears with the fuller measure of Divine inspiration for the next stage in the awakening and civilizing of humankind.

Consider the hour at which the supreme Manifestation of God revealeth Himself unto men. Ere that hour cometh, the Ancient Being, Who is still unknown of men and hath not as yet given utterance to the Word of God, is Himself the All-Knower in a world devoid of any man that hath known Him. He is indeed the Creator without a creation ... This is indeed the Day of which it hath been written: "Whose shall be the

Kingdom this Day?" And none can be found ready to answer![52]

Until a section of humanity begins to respond to the new Revelation, and a new spiritual and social paradigm begins to take shape, people subsist spiritually and morally on the last traces of earlier Divine endowments. The routine tasks of society may or may not be done; laws may be obeyed or flouted; social and political experimentation may flame up or fail; but the roots of faith — without which no society can indefinitely endure — have been exhausted. At the "end of the age," at the "end of the world," the spiritually minded begin to turn again to the Creative source. However clumsy or disturbing the process may be, however inelegant or unfortunate some of the options considered, such searching is an instinctive response to the awareness that an immense chasm has opened in the ordered life of humankind.[53] The effects of the new Revelation, Bahá'u'lláh says, are universal, and not limited to the life and teachings of the Manifestation of God Who is the Revelation's focal point. Though not understood, these effects increasingly permeate human affairs, revealing the contradictions in popular assumptions and in society, and intensifying the search for understanding.

The succession of the Manifestations is an inseparable dimension of existence, Bahá'u'lláh declares, and will continue throughout the life of the world: "*God hath sent down His Messengers to succeed to Moses and Jesus, and He will continue to do so till 'the end that hath no end'...*"[54]

The Day of God

What does Bahá'u'lláh hold to be the goal of the evolution of human consciousness? In the perspective of eternity, its purpose is that God should see, ever more clearly, the reflection of His perfections in the mirror of His creation, and that, in the words of Bahá'u'lláh:

> ... every man may testify, in himself, by himself, in the station of the Manifestation of his Lord, that verily there is no God save Him, and that every man may thereby win his way to the summit of realities, until none shall contemplate anything whatsoever but that he shall see God therein.[55]

Within the context of the history of civilization, the objective of the succession of Divine Manifestations has been to prepare human consciousness for the race's unification as a single species, indeed as a single organism capable of taking up the responsibility for its collective future: "*He Who is your Lord, the All-Merciful,*" Bahá'u'lláh says, "*cherisheth in His heart the desire of beholding the entire human race as one soul and one body.*"[56] Not until humanity has accepted its organic oneness can it meet even its immediate challenges, let alone those that lie ahead: "*The well-being of mankind,*" Bahá'u'lláh insists, "*its peace and security, are unattainable unless and until its unity is firmly established.*"[57] Only a unified global society can provide its children with the sense of inner assurance implied in one of Bahá'u'lláh's prayers to God: "*Whatever duty Thou hast prescribed unto Thy servants of extolling to the utmost Thy majesty and glory is but a token of Thy grace unto them, that they may be enabled to ascend unto the station conferred upon their own inmost being, the station of the knowledge of their own selves.*"[58] Paradoxically, it is only by achieving true unity that humanity can fully cultivate its diversity and individuality. This is the goal which the missions of all the Manifestations of God known to history have served, the Day of "one fold and one shepherd."[59] Its attainment, Bahá'u'lláh says, is the stage of civilization upon which the human race is now entering.

One of the most suggestive analogies to be found in the writings not only of Bahá'u'lláh, but of the Báb before Him, is the comparison between the evolution of the human race and the life of the individual human being. Humanity has moved through the stages in its collective development which are reminiscent of the periods of infancy, childhood, and adolescence in the maturation of its individual members. We are now experiencing the beginnings of our collective maturity, endowed with new capacities and opportunities of which we as yet have only the dimmest awareness.[60]

Against this background, it is not difficult to understand the primacy given in Bahá'u'lláh's teachings to the principle of unity. The oneness of humanity is the leitmotif of the age now opening, the standard against which must be tested all proposals for the betterment of humanity. There is, Bahá'u'lláh insists, but one human race; inherited notions that a particular racial or ethnic group is in some way superior to the rest of humanity are without foundation. Similarly, since all of the Messengers of God have served as agents of the one Divine Will, their Revelations are the collective legacy of the entire human race; each person on earth is a legitimate heir of the whole of that spiritual tradition. Persistence in prejudices of any kind is both damaging to the interests of society and a violation of the Will of God for our age:

> O contending peoples and kindreds of the earth! Set your faces towards unity, and let the radiance of its light shine upon you. Gather ye together, and for the sake of God resolve to root out whatever is the source of contention amongst you ... There can be no doubt whatever that the peoples of the world, of whatever race or religion, derive their inspiration from one heavenly Source, and are the subjects of one God. The difference between the ordinances under which they abide should be attributed to the varying requirements and exigencies of the age in which they were revealed. All of them, except a few which are the outcome of human perversity, were ordained of God, and are a reflection of His Will and Purpose. Arise and, armed with the power of faith, shatter to pieces the gods of your vain imaginings, the sowers of dissension amongst you ...[61]

The theme of unity runs throughout Bahá'u'lláh's writings: "*The tabernacle of unity hath been raised; regard ye not one another as strangers.*" [62] "*Consort with the followers of all religions in a spirit of friendliness and fellowship.*" [63] "*Ye are the fruits of one tree, and the leaves of one branch.*" [64]

The process of humanity's coming-of-age has occurred within the evolution of social organization. Beginning from the family unit and its various extensions, the human race has developed, with varying degrees of success, societies based on the clan, the tribe, the city-state, and most recently the nation. This progressively broader and more complex social milieu provides human potential with both stimulation and scope for development, and this development, in turn, has induced ever-new modifications of the social fabric. Humanity's coming-of-age, therefore, must entail a total transformation of the social order. The new society must be one capable of embracing the entire diversity of the race and of benefiting from the full range of talents and insights which many thousands of years of cultural experience have refined:

> This is the Day in which God's most excellent favors have been poured out upon men, the Day in which His most mighty grace hath been infused into all created things. It is incumbent upon all the peoples of the world to reconcile their differences, and, with the perfect unity and peace, abide beneath the shadow of the Tree of His care and loving-kindness ... Soon will the present-day order be rolled up, and a new one spread out in its stead. Verily, thy Lord speaketh the truth, and is the Knower of things unseen.[65]

The chief instrument for the transformation of society and the achievement of world unity, Bahá'u'lláh asserts, is the establishment of justice in the affairs of humankind. The subject has a central place in His teachings:

> The light of men is Justice. Quench it not with the contrary winds of oppression and tyranny. The purpose of justice is the appearance of unity among men. The ocean of divine wisdom surgeth within this exalted word, while the books of the world cannot contain its inner significance ...[66]

In His later writings Bahá'u'lláh made explicit the implications of this principle for the

37

age of humanity's maturity. "*Women and men have been and will always be equal in the sight of God*,"[67] He asserts, and the advancement of civilization requires that society so organize its affairs as to give full expression to this fact. The earth's resources are the property of all humanity, not of any one people. Different contributions to the common economic welfare deserve and should receive different measures of reward and recognition, but the extremes of wealth and poverty which afflict most nations on earth, regardless of the socio-economic philosophies they profess, must be abolished.

*A*nnouncement to the Kings

The writings which have been quoted in the foregoing were revealed, for the most part, in conditions of renewed persecution. Soon after the exiles' arrival in Constantinople, it became apparent that the honors showered upon Bahá'u'lláh during His journey from Baghdad had represented only a brief interlude. The Ottoman authorities' decision to move the "Bábí" leader and His companions to the capital of the empire rather than to some remote province deepened the alarm among the representatives of the Persian government.[68] Fearing that the developments in Baghdad would be repeated, and might attract this time not only the sympathy but perhaps even the allegiance of influential figures in the Turkish government, the Persian ambassador pressed insistently for the dispatch of the exiles to some more distant part of the empire. His argument was that the spread of a new religious message in the capital could produce political as well as religious repercussions.

Initially, the Ottoman government strongly resisted. The chief minister, 'Alí Páshá, had indicated to Western diplomats his belief that Bahá'u'lláh was "a man of great distinction, exemplary conduct, great moderation, and a most dignified figure." His teachings were, in the minister's opinion, "worthy of high esteem" because they counteracted the religious animosities dividing the Jewish, Christian, and Muslim subjects of the empire.[69]

Gradually, however, a degree of resentment and suspicion developed. In the

39

Ottoman capital, political and economic power was in the hands of court functionaries who, with but few exceptions, were persons of little or no competence. Venality was the oil on which the machinery of government operated, and the capital was a magnet for a horde of people who flocked there from every part of the empire and beyond, seeking favors and influence. It was expected that any prominent figure from another country or from one of the tribute territories would, immediately upon arrival in Constantinople, join the throngs of patronage-seekers in the reception rooms of the pashas and ministers of the imperial court. No element had a worse reputation than the competing groups of Persian political exiles who were known for both their sophistication and their lack of scruple.

To the distress of friends who urged Him to make use of the prevailing hostility toward the Persian government and of the sympathy which His own sufferings had aroused, Bahá'u'lláh made it clear that He had no requests to make. Although several government ministers made social calls at the residence assigned to Him, he did not take advantage of these openings. He was in Constantinople, He said, as the guest of the Sultan, at his invitation, and His interest lay in spiritual and moral concerns.

Many years later, the Persian ambassador, Mírzá Husayn Khán, reflecting on his tour of duty in the Ottoman capital, and complaining about the damage which the greed and untrustworthiness of his countrymen had done to Persia's reputation in Constantinople, paid a surprisingly candid tribute to the example which Bahá'u'lláh's conduct had been able briefly to set.[70] At the time, however, he and his colleagues made use of the situation to represent it as an astute way on the exile's part of concealing secret conspiracies against public security and the religion of the State. Under pressure of these influences, the Ottoman authorities finally took the decision to transfer Bahá'u'lláh and His family to the provincial city of Adrianople. The move was made hastily, in the depth of an extremely severe winter. Housed there in inadequate buildings, lacking suitable clothing and other provisions, the exiles endured a year of great suffering. It was clear that, though charged with no crime and given no opportunity to defend themselves, they had arbitrarily been made state prisoners.

From the point of view of religious history, the successive banishments of Bahá'u'lláh to Constantinople and Adrianople have a striking symbolism. For the first time, a Manifestation of God, Founder of an independent religious system which was soon to spread throughout the planet, had crossed the narrow neck of water separating Asia from Europe, and had set foot in "the West." All of the other great religions had arisen in Asia, and the ministries of their Founders had been confined to that continent. Referring to the fact that the dispensations of the past, and particularly those of Abraham, Christ, and Muḥammad, had produced their most important effects on the development of civilization during the course of their westward expansion, Bahá'u'lláh predicted that the same thing would occur in this new age, but on a vastly larger scale: "*In the East the Light of His Revelation hath broken; in the West the signs of His dominion have appeared. Ponder this in your hearts, O people ...*"[71]

It is then perhaps not surprising that Bahá'u'lláh chose this moment to make public the mission which had been slowly enlisting the allegiance of the followers of the Báb throughout the Middle East. His announcement took the form of a series of statements which are among the most remarkable documents in religious history. In them, the Manifestation of God addresses the "Kings and Rulers of the world," announcing to them the dawning of the Day of God, alluding to the as yet inconceivable changes which were gathering momentum throughout the world, and calling on them as the trustees of God and of their fellow human beings to arise and serve the process of the unification of the human race. Because of the veneration in which they were held by the mass of their subjects, and because of the absolute nature of the rule which most of them exercised, it lay in their power, He said, to assist in bringing about what He called the "*Most Great Peace*," a world order characterized by unity and animated by Divine justice.

Only with the greatest difficulty can the modern reader envision the moral and intellectual world in which these monarchs of a century ago lived. From their biographies and private correspondence, it is apparent that, with few exceptions, they were personally devout, taking a leading part in the spiritual life of their respective nations, often as the heads of the state religions, and convinced of the unerring truths of the Bible or the Qur'án. The power which most of them wielded they attributed directly to the Divine authority of passages in these same scriptures, an authority about which they were vigorously articulate. They were the anointed of God. Prophecies of "the Latter Days" and "the Kingdom of God" were not for them myth or allegory, but certainties upon which all moral order rested and in which they would themselves be called on by God to give an account of their stewardship.

The letters of Bahá'u'lláh address themselves to this mental world:

> O Kings of the earth! He Who is the sovereign Lord of all is come. The Kingdom is God's, the omnipotent Protector, the Self-Subsisting ... This is a Revelation to which whatever ye possess can never be compared, could ye but know it ...

> ... Take heed lest pride deter you from recognizing the Source of Revelation, lest the things of this world shut you out as by a veil from Him Who is the Creator of heaven ... By the righteousness of God! It is not Our wish to lay hands on your kingdoms. Our mission is to seize and possess the hearts of men ...[72]

> Know ye that the poor are the trust of God in your midst. Watch that ye betray not His trust, that ye deal not unjustly with them and that ye walk not in the ways of the treacherous. Ye will most certainly be called upon to answer for His trust on the day when the Balance of Justice shall be set, the day when unto every one shall be rendered his due, when the doings of all men, be they rich or poor, shall be weighed ...

> Examine Our Cause, inquire into the things that have befallen Us, and decide justly between Us and Our enemies, and be ye of them that act equitably towards their neighbor. If ye stay not the hand of the oppressor, if ye fail to safeguard the rights of the downtrodden, what right have ye then to vaunt yourselves among men?[73] ...

> If ye pay no heed unto the counsels which ... We have revealed in this Tablet, Divine chastisement shall assail you from every direction, and the sentence of His justice shall be pronounced against you. On that day ye shall have no power to resist Him, and shall recognize your own impotence ...[74]

The vision of the "Most Great Peace" evoked no response from the rulers of the nineteenth century. Nationalistic aggrandizement and imperial expansion recruited not only kings but parliamentarians, academics, artists, newspapers, and the major religious establishments as eager propagandists of Western triumphalism. Proposals for social change, however disinterested and idealistic, quickly fell captive to a swarm of new ideologies thrown up by the rising tide of dogmatic materialism. In the Orient, mesmerized by its own claims to represent all that humanity ever could or would know of God and truth, the Islamic world sank steadily deeper into ignorance, lethargy, and a sullen hostility to a human race which failed to acknowledge this spiritual preeminence.

Arrival in the Holy Land

Given the earlier events in Baghdad, it seems surprising that the Ottoman authorities did not anticipate what would result from the establishment of Bahá'u'lláh in another major provincial capital. Within a year of His arrival in Adrianople, their prisoner had attracted first the interest and then the fervent admiration of figures prominent in both the intellectual and administrative life of the region. To the dismay of the Persian consular representatives, two of the most devoted of these admirers where Khurshíd Páshá, the governor of the province, and the Shaykhu'l-Islám, the leading Sunni religious dignitary. In the eyes of His hosts and the public generally, the exile was a moral philosopher and saint the validity of whose teachings was reflected not only in the example of His own life but in the changes they effected among the flood of Persian pilgrims who flocked to this remote center of the Ottoman Empire in order to visit Him.[75]

These unanticipated developments convinced the Persian ambassador and his colleagues that it was only a matter of time before the Bahá'í movement, which was continuing to spread in Persia, would have established itself as a major influence in Persia's neighboring and rival empire. Throughout this period of its history, the ramshackle Ottoman Empire was struggling against repeated incursions by Tsarist Russia, uprisings among its subject peoples, and persistent attempts by the ostensibly sympathetic British and Austrian governments to detach various Turkish territories and incorporate them into their own empires. These unstable political

45

conditions in Turkey's European provinces offered new and urgent arguments supporting the ambassador's appeal that the exiles be sent to a distant colony where Bahá'u'lláh would have no further contact with influential circles, whether Turkish or Western.

When the Turkish foreign minister, Fu'ád Páshá, returned from a visit to Adrianople, his astonished reports of the reputation which Bahá'u'lláh had come to enjoy throughout the region appeared to lend credibility to the Persian embassy's suggestions. In this climate of opinion, the government abruptly decided to subject its guest to strict confinement. Without warning, early one day, Bahá'u'lláh's house was surrounded by soldiers, and the exiles were ordered to prepare for departure to an unknown destination.

The place chosen for this final banishment was the grim fortress-town of Akká (Acre) on the coast of the Holy Land. Notorious throughout the empire for the foulness of its climate and the prevalence of many diseases, Akka was a penal colony used by the Ottoman State for the incarceration of dangerous criminals who could be expected not to survive too long their imprisonment there. Arriving in August 1868, Bahá'u'lláh, the members of His family, and a company of His followers who had been exiled with Him were to experience two years of suffering and abuse within the fortress itself, and then be confined under house arrest to a nearby building owned by a local merchant. For a long time the exiles were shunned by the superstitious local populace who had been warned in public sermons against "the God of the Persians," who was depicted as an enemy of public order and the purveyor of blasphemous and immoral ideas.

Several members of the small group of exiles died of the privations and other conditions to which they were subjected.[76]

It seems, in retrospect, the keenest irony that the selection of the Holy Land as the place of Bahá'u'lláh's forced confinement should have been the result of pressure from ecclesiastical and civil enemies whose aim was to extinguish His religious influence. Palestine, revered by three of the great monotheistic religions as the point where the worlds of God and of man intersect, held then, as it had for thousands of years, a unique place in human expectation. Only a few weeks before Bahá'u'lláh's arrival, the main leadership of the German Protestant Templer movement sailed from Europe to establish at the foot of Mount Carmel a colony that would welcome Christ, whose advent they believed to be imminent. Over the lintels of several of the small houses they erected, facing across the bay to Bahá'u'lláh's prison at Akká, can still be seen such carved inscriptions as "*Der Herr ist nahe* " ("The Lord is near").[77]

In Akká, Bahá'u'lláh continued the dictation of a series of letters to individual rulers, which He had begun in Adrianople. Several contained warnings of the judgment of God on their negligence and misrule, warnings whose dramatic fulfillment aroused intense public discussion throughout the Near East. Less than two months after the exiles arrived in the prison-city, for example, Fu'ád Páshá, the Ottoman foreign minister, whose misrepresentations had helped precipitate the banishment, was abruptly dismissed from his post and died in France of a heart attack. The event was marked by a statement which predicted the early dismissal of his colleague, Prime Minister 'Alí Páshá, the overthrow and death of the Sultan, and the loss of Turkish territories in Europe, a series of disasters which followed on the heels of one another.[78]

A letter to Emperor Napoleon III warned that, because of his insincerity and the misuse of his power: "... *thy kingdom shall be thrown into confusion, and thine empire shall pass from thine hands, as a punishment for that which thou has wrought.... Hath thy pomp made thee proud? By My life! It shall not endure...*"[79] Of the disastrous Franco-Prussian War and the resulting overthrow of Napoleon III, which occurred less than a year after this statement, Alistair Horne, a modern scholar of nineteenth century French Political History has written:

> History knows of perhaps no more startling instance of what the Greeks called *peripateia*, the terrible fall from prideful heights. Certainly no nation in modern times, so replete with apparent grandeur and opulent in material achievement, has ever been subjected to a worse humiliation in so short a time.[80]

Only a few months before the unexpected series of events in Europe that led to the invasion of the Papal States and the annexation of Rome by the forces of the new Kingdom of Italy, a statement addressing Pope Pius IX had urged the Pontiff, "*Abandon thy kingdom unto the kings, and emerge from thy habitation, with thy face set towards the Kingdom... Be as thy Lord hath been.... Verily, the day of ingathering is come, and all things have been separated from each other. He hath stored away that which He chose in the vessels of justice, and cast into the fire that which befitteth it....*"[81]

Particularly ominous was a passage in the writings of this same period, envisioning more distant events in Germany. The Prussian king, Wilhelm I, whose government had deliberately provoked the war that had led to the crushing defeat of France and to the creation of a new "German Empire," was warned:

> O banks of the Rhine! We have seen you covered with gore, inasmuch as the swords of retribution were drawn against you; and you shall have another turn. And We hear the lamentations of Berlin, though she be today in conspicuous glory.[82]

A strikingly different note characterizes two of the major pronouncements — that addressed to Queen Victoria[83] and another to the "Rulers of America and the Presidents of the Republics therein." The former praises the pioneering achievement represented by the abolition of slavery throughout the British Empire, and commends the principle of representative government. The latter, which opens with the announcement of the Day of God, concludes with a summons, a virtual mandate, that has no parallel in any of the other messages: "*Bind ye the broken with the hands of justice, and crush the oppressor who flourisheth with the rod of the commandments of your Lord, the Ordainer, the All-Wise.*"[84]

Religion as Light and Darkness

Bahá'u'lláh's severest condemnation is reserved for the barriers which, throughout history, organised religion has erected between humanity and the Revelations of God. Dogmas, inspired by popular superstition and perfected by misspent intelligence, have repeatedly been imposed on a Divine process whose purpose has at all times been spiritual and moral. Laws of social interaction, revealed for the purpose of consolidating community life, have been made the basis for structures of arcane doctrine and practice which have burdened the masses whose benefit they were supposed to serve. Even the exercise of intellect, the chief tool possessed by the human race, has been deliberately hampered, producing an eventual breakdown in the dialogue between faith and science upon which civilized life depends.

The consequence of this sorry record is the worldwide disrepute into which religion has fallen. Worse, organized religion has become itself a most virulent cause of hatred and warfare among the peoples of the world. "*Religious fanaticism and hatred,*" Bahá'u'lláh warned over a century ago, "*are a world-devouring fire, whose violence none can quench. The Hand of Divine power can, alone, deliver mankind from this desolating affliction.*"[85]

Those whom God will hold responsible for this tragedy, Bahá'u'lláh says, are humanity's religious leaders, who have presumed to speak for Him throughout history. Their attempts to make the Word of God a private preserve, and its exposition a means for personal aggrandizement, have been the greatest single handicap against which the advancement of civilization has struggled. In the pursuit of their ends, many of them have not hesitated to raise their hands against the Messengers of God themselves, at their advent:

> Leaders of religion, in every age, have hindered their people from attaining the shores of eternal salvation, inasmuch as they held the reins of authority in their mighty grasp. Some for the lust of leadership, others through want of knowledge and understanding, have been the cause of the deprivation of the people. By their sanction and authority, every Prophet of God hath drunk from the chalice of sacrifice...[86]

In an address to the clergy of all faiths, Bahá'u'lláh warns of the responsibility which they have so carelessly assumed in history:

> Ye are even as a spring. If it be changed, so will the streams that branch out from it be changed. Fear God, and be numbered with the godly. In like manner, if the heart of man be corrupted, his limbs will also be corrupted. And similarly, if the root of a tree be corrupted, its branches, and its offshoots, and its leaves, and its fruits, will be corrupted.[87]

These same statements, revealed at a time when religious orthodoxy was one of the major powers throughout the world, declared that this power had effectively ended, and that the ecclesiastical caste has no further social role in world history: "*O concourse of divines! Ye shall not henceforward behold yourselves possessed of any power...*"[88] To a particularly vindictive opponent among the Muslim clergy, Bahá'u'lláh said: "*Thou art even as the last trace of sunlight upon the mountaintop. Soon will it fade away as decreed by God, the All-Possessing, the Most High. Thy glory and the glory of such as are like thee have been taken away...* [89]

It is not the organization of religious activity which these statements address, but the misuse of such resources. Bahá'u'lláh's writings are generous in their appreciation not only of the great contribution which organized religion has brought to civilization, but also of the benefits which the world has derived from the self-sacrifice and love of humanity that have characterized clergymen and religious orders of all faiths:

Those divines ... who are truly adorned with the ornament of knowledge and of a goodly character are, verily as a head to the body of the world, and as eyes to the nations.... [90]

Rather, the challenge to all people, believers and unbelievers, clergy and laymen alike, is to recognize the consequences now being visited upon the world as the result of the universal corruption of the religious impulse. In the prevailing alienation of humanity from God over the past century, a relationship on which the fabric of moral life itself depends has broken down. Natural faculties of the rational soul, vital to the development and maintenance of human values, have become universally discounted:

The vitality of men's belief in God is dying out in every land; nothing short of His wholesome medicine can ever restore it. The corrosion of ungodliness is eating into the vitals of human society; what else but the Elixir of His potent Revelation can cleanse and revive it?... The Word of God, alone, can claim the distinction of being endowed with the capacity required for so great and far-reaching a change. [91]

*W*orld Peace

In the light of subsequent events, the warnings and appeals of Bahá'u'lláh's writings during this period take on a terrible poignancy:

O ye the elected representatives of the people in every land!... Regard the world as the human body which, though at its creation whole and perfect, hath been afflicted, through various causes, with grave disorders and maladies. Not for one day did it gain ease, nay its sickness waxed more severe, as it fell under the treatment of ignorant physicians, who gave full rein to their personal desires...

We behold it, in this day, at the mercy of rulers so drunk with pride that they cannot discern clearly their own best advantage, much less recognize a Revelation so bewildering and challenging as this....[92]

This is the Day whereon the earth shall tell out her tidings. The workers of iniquity are her burdens, could ye but perceive it....[93]

All men have been created to carry forward an ever-advancing civilization. The Almighty beareth Me witness: To act like the beasts of the field is unworthy of man. Those virtues that befit his dignity are forbearance, mercy, compassion and loving-kindness towards all the peoples and kindreds of the earth....[94]

A new life is, in this age, stirring within all the peoples of the earth; and yet none hath discovered its cause or perceived its motive. Consider the peoples of the West. Witness how, in their pursuit of that which is vain and trivial,

*they have sacrificed, and are still sacrificing,
countless lives for the sake of its establishment
and promotion....*[95]

*In all matters moderation is desirable. If a thing
is carried to excess, it will prove a source of
evil.... Strange and astonishing things exist in the
earth but they are hidden from the minds and
the understanding of men. These things are
capable of changing the whole atmosphere of
the earth and their contamination would prove
lethal....*[96]

In later writings, including those addressed
to humanity collectively, Bahá'u'lláh urged the
adoption of steps toward what He called the
"Great Peace." These, He said, would mitigate the
sufferings and dislocation which He saw lying
ahead of the human race until the world's peoples
embrace the Revelation of God and through it
bring about the Most Great Peace:

*The time must come when the imperative
necessity for the holding of a vast, an
all-embracing assemblage of men will be
universally realized. The rulers and kings of the
earth must needs attend it, and, participating in
its deliberations, must consider such ways and
means as will lay the foundations of the world's
Great Peace amongst men. Such a peace
demandeth that the Great Powers should resolve
for the sake of the tranquility of the peoples of
the earth, to be fully reconciled among
themselves. Should any king take up arms
against another, all should unitedly arise and
prevent him. If this be done, the nations of the
world will no longer require any armaments,
except for the purpose of preserving the security
of their realms and of maintaining internal order
within their territories.... The day is approaching
when all the peoples of the world will have*

adopted one universal language and one common script. When this is achieved, to whatsoever city a man may journey, it shall be as if he were entering his own home.... That one indeed is a man who, today, dedicateth himself to the service of the entire human race.... It is not for him to pride himself who loveth his own country, but rather for him who loveth the whole world. The earth is but one country, and mankind its citizens.[97]

Not of Mine Own Volition

In His letter to Násiri'd-Dín Sháh, the ruler of Persia, which refrains from any rebuke concerning His imprisonment in the Síyáh-Chál and the other injustices He had experienced at the king's hand, Bahá'u'lláh speaks of His own role in the Divine Plan:

> *I was but a man like others, asleep upon My couch, when lo, the breezes of the All-Glorious were wafted over Me, and taught Me the knowledge of all that hath been. This thing is not from Me, but from One Who is Almighty and All-Knowing. And He bade Me lift up My voice between earth and heaven, and for this there befell Me what hath caused the tears of every man of understanding to flow. The learning current amongst men I studied not; their schools I entered not. Ask of the city wherein I dwelt, that thou mayest be well assured that I am not of them who speak falsely.[98]*

The mission to which He had devoted His entire life, which had cost Him the life of a cherished younger son[99], as well as all of His material possessions, which had undermined His health, and brought imprisonment, exile, and abuse, was not one that He had initiated. "*Not of Mine own volition*," He said, had He entered on such a course:

> *Think ye, O people, that I hold within My grasp the control of God's ultimate Will and Purpose?... Had the ultimate destiny of God's Faith been in Mine hands, I would have never consented, even though for one moment, to*

manifest Myself unto you, nor would I have allowed one word to fall from My lips. Of this God Himself is, verily, a witness.[100]

Having surrendered unreservedly to God's summons, He was in no doubt about the role which He had been called upon to play in human history. As the Manifestation of God to the age of fulfillment, He is the one promised in all the scriptures of the past, the "Desire of nations," the "King of Glory." To Judaism He is "Lord of Hosts"; to Christianity, the Return of Christ in the glory of the Father; to Islam, the "Great Announcement"; to Buddhism, the Maitreya Buddha; to Hinduism, the new incarnation of Krishna; to Zoroastrianism, the advent of "Sháh-Bahrám."[101]

Like the Manifestations of God gone before Him, He is both the Voice of God and its human channel: *"When I contemplate, O my God, the relationship that bindeth me to Thee, I am moved to proclaim to all created things 'verily I am God!'; and when I consider my own self, lo, I find it coarser than clay!"*[102]

"Certain ones among you," He declared, *"have said: 'He it is Who hath laid claim to be God.' By God! This is a gross calumny. I am but a servant of God Who hath believed in Him and in His signs... My tongue, and My heart, and My inner and My outer being testify that there is no God but Him, that all others have been created by His behest, and been fashioned through the operation of His Will.... I am He that telleth abroad the favors with which God hath, through His bounty, favored Me. If this be My transgression, then I am truly the first of the transgressors...."*[103]

Bahá'u'lláh's writings seize upon a host of metaphors in their attempt to express the paradox

57

that lies at the heart of the phenomenon of God's Revelation of His Will:

> I am the royal Falcon on the arm of the Almighty. I unfold the drooping wings of every broken bird and start it on its flight.[104]

> This is but a leaf which the winds of the will of thy Lord, the Almighty, the All-Praised, have stirred. Can it be still when the tempestuous winds are blowing? Nay, by Him Who is the Lord of all Names and Attributes! They move it as they list....[105]

The Covenant of God with Humankind

In June 1877, Bahá'u'lláh at last emerged from the strict confinement of the prison-city of Akká, and moved with His family to "Mazra'ih," a small estate a few miles north of the city.[106] As had been predicted in His statement to the Turkish government, Sultán 'Abdu'l-'Azíz had been overthrown and assassinated in a palace coup, and gusts from the winds of political change sweeping the world were beginning to invade even the shuttered precincts of the Ottoman imperial system. After a brief two-year stay at Mazra'ih, Bahá'u'lláh moved to "Bahjí", a large mansion surrounded by gardens, which His son 'Abdu'l-Bahá had rented for Him and the members of His extended family.[107] The remaining twelve years of His life were devoted to His writings on a wide range of spiritual and social issues, and to receiving a stream of Bahá'í pilgriims who made their way, with great difficulty, from Persia and other lands.

Throughout the Near and Middle East the nucleus of a community life was beginning to take shape among those who had accepted His message. For its guidance, Bahá'u'lláh had revealed a system of laws and institutions designed to give practical effect to the principles in His writings.[108] Authority was vested in councils democratically elected by the whole community, provisions were made to exclude the possibility of a clerical elite arising, and principles of consultation and group decision making were established.

At the heart of this system was what Bahá'u'lláh termed a "new Covenant" between God and humankind. The distinguishing feature of humanity's coming of age is that, for the first time in its history, the entire human race is consciously involved, however dimly, in the awareness of its own oneness and of the earth as a single homeland. This awakening opens the way to a new relationship between God and humankind. As the peoples of the world embrace the spiritual authority inherent in the guidance of the Revelation of God for this age, Bahá'u'lláh said, they will find in themselves a moral empowerment which human effort alone has proven incapable of generating. "A new race of men"[109] will emerge as the result of this relationship, and the work of building a global civilization will begin. The mission of the Bahá'í community is to demonstrate the efficacy of this Covenant in healing the ills that divide the human race.

Bahá'u'lláh died at Bahjí on May 29, 1892, in His seventy-fifth year. At the time of His passing, the cause entrusted to Him forty years earlier in the darkness of Teheran's Black Pit was poised to break free of the Islamic lands where it had taken shape, and to establish itself first across America and Europe and then throughout the world. In doing so, it would itself become a vindication of the promise of the new Covenant between God and humankind. For alone of all the world's independent religions, the Bahá'í Faith and its community of believers were to pass successfully through the critical first century of their existence with their unity firmly intact, undamaged by the age-old blight of schism and faction. Their experience offers compelling evidence for Bahá'u'lláh's assurance that the human race, in all its diversity, can learn to live and work as one people, in a common global homeland.

Just two years before His death, Bahá'u'lláh received at Bahjí one of the few Westerners to meet Him, and the only one to leave a written account of the experience. The visitor was Edward Granville Browne, a rising young orientalist from Cambridge University, whose attention had originally been attracted by the dramatic history of the Báb and His heroic band of followers. Of his meeting with Bahá'u'lláh, Browne wrote:

Though I dimly suspected whither I was going and whom I was to behold (for no distinct intimation had been given to me), a second or two elapsed ere, with a throb of wonder and awe, I became definitely conscious that the room was not untenanted. In the corner where the divan met the wall sat a wondrous and venerable figure.... The face of him on whom I gazed I can never forget, though I cannot describe it. Those piercing eyes seemed to read one's very soul; power and authority sat on that ample brow... No need to ask in whose presence I stood, as I bowed myself before one who is the object of a devotion and love which kings might envy and emperors sigh for in vain! A mild dignified voice bade me be seated, and then continued: _ "Praise be to God that thou hast attained!... Thou hast come to see a prisoner and an exile... We desire but the good of the world and the happiness of the nations; yet they deem us a stirrer up of strife and sedition worthy of bondage and banishment... That all nations should become one in faith and all men as brothers; that the bonds of affection and unity between the sons of men should be strengthened; that diversity of religion should

61

cease, and differences of race be annulled _
what harm is there in this?... Yet so it shall be;
these fruitless strifes, these ruinous wars shall
pass away, and the 'Most great Peace' shall
come..."[110]

NOTES

1.   Bahá'u'lláh ("Glory of God") was born
      Ḥusayn-'Alí. The authoritative work on the
      missions of the Báb and Bahá'u'lláh is
      Shoghi Effendi's *God Passes By* (Wilmette:
      Bahá'í Publishing Trust, 1987). For a
      biographical study see Hasan Balyuzi's
      Bahá'u'lláh: The King of Glory (Oxford:
      George Ronald, 1980). Bahá'u'lláh's
      writings are extensively reviewed in Adib
      Taherzadeh's *The Revelation of Bahá'u'lláh*
      (Oxford: George Ronald, 1975), four
      volumes.

2.   *Britannica Yearbook*, 1988, indicates that,
      although the Bahá'í community numbers
      only about five million members, the Faith
      has already become the most widely
      diffused religion on earth, after Christianity.
      There are today 155 Bahá'í National
      Assemblies in independent countries and
      major territories of the globe, and more
      than 17,000 elected Assemblies
      functioning at the local level. It is estimated
      that 2,112 nationalities and tribes are
      represented.

3.   Arnold Toynbee, *A Study of History*, Vol.
      VIII (London: Oxford, 1954), p. 117.

4.   The Báb ("Gate" or "Door") was born Siyyid
      'Alí-Muḥammad in Shiraz, October 20,
      1819.

5.   Passages in the Báb's writings which refer
      to the advent of "*Him Whom God will
      make manifest*" include cryptic references

to "*the year Nine*" and "*the year Nineteen*" (i.e., roughly 1852 and 1863, calculating in lunar years from the year of the Báb's inauguration of His mission, 1844). On several occasions the Báb also indicated to certain of His followers that they would themselves come to recognize and serve "*Him Whom God will make manifest.*"

6. The proclamation of the Báb's message had been carried out in mosques and public places by enthusiastic bands of followers, many of them young seminarians. The Muslim clergy had replied by inciting mob violence. Unfortunately, these events coincided with a political crisis created by the death of Muḥammad S͟háh and a struggle over the succession. It was the leaders of the successful political faction, behind the boy-king Náṣiri'd-Din S͟háh, who then turned the royal army against the Bábí enthusiasts. The latter, raised in a Muslim frame of reference, and believing that they had a moral right to self-defense, barricaded themselves in makeshift shelters and withstood long, bloody sieges. When they had eventually been overcome and slaughtered, and the Báb had been executed, two deranged Bábí youth stopped the Shah in a public road and fired birdshot at him in an ill-conceived attempt at assassination. It was this incident which provided the excuse for the worst of the massacres of Bábís which evoked protests from Western embassies. For an account of the period see W. Hatcher and D. Martin, *The Bahá'í Faith: The Emerging Global Religion* (San Francisco: Harper and Row, 1985), pp. 6-32.

7. For an account of these events see *God Passes By*, chapters I-V. Western interest in the Bábí movement was aroused, particularly, by the publication in 1865 of Joseph Arthur Comte de Gobineau's *Les religions et les philosophies dans l'Asie centrale* (Paris: Didier, 1865).

8. Bahá'u'lláh, *Epistle to the Son of the Wolf* (Wilmette, Ill.: Bahá'í Publishing Trust, 1979), pp. 20-21.

9. A number of Western diplomatic and military observers have left harrowing accounts of what they witnessed. Several formal protests were registered with the Persian authorities. See Moojan Momen, *The Bábí and Bahá'í Religions, 1844-1944* (Oxford: George Ronald, 1981).

10. *Epistle*, p. 21.

11. *Epistle*, p. 22.

12. There was, understandably, great suspicion in Persia about the intentions of the British and Russian governments, both of which had long interfered in Persian affairs.

13. The focal point of these problems was one Mírzá Yaḥyá, a younger half-brother of Bahá'u'lláh. While still a youth and under the guidance of Bahá'u'lláh Yaḥyá had been appointed by the Báb as nominal head of the Bábí community, pending the imminent advent of "Him Whom God will make manifest." Falling under the influence of a former Muslim theologian, Siyyid Muḥammad Iṣfahání, however, Yaḥyá gradually became estranged from his brother. Rather than being expressed openly, this resentment found its outlet in clandestine agitation, which had a disastrous effect on the exiles' already low

morale. Yaḥyá eventually refused to accept Bahá'u'lláh's declaration, and played no role in the development of the Bahá'í Faith which this declaration initiated.

14. Bahá'u'lláh, *The Book of Certitude* (Wilmette, Ill.: Bahá'í Publishing Trust, 1985), p. 251.

15. Bahá'u'lláh, *The Hidden Words* (Wilmette, Ill.: Bahá'í Publishing Trust, 1985), Arabic 2 on pp.3-4, Arabic 5 on p. 4, Arabic 35 on p. 12, Arabic 12 on p. 6.
    Except where the context makes it obvious, the conventional use of the English word "man" translates the concept of "humanity."

16. *Certitude*, pp. 3-4, pp. 195-96, 197, 199-200.

17. Cited in *God Passes By*, p. 137.

18. Quotation from Prince Zaynu'l-Abidín Khán, *God Passes By*, p. 135.

19. See Note 68 below.

20. *God Passes By*, p. 153. Increasingly, after 1863, the word "Bahá'í" replaced "Bábí" as the designation for the new faith, marking the fact that an entirely new religion had emerged.

21. Cited in Shoghi Effendi, *The Advent of Divine Justice* (Wilmette, Ill.: Bahá'í Publishing Trust, 1984), p. 77.

22. Bahá'u'lláh, *Gleanings from the Writings of Bahá'u'lláh* (Wilmette, Ill.: Bahá'í Publishing Trust, 1983), pp. 10-11.

23. *Gleanings*, p. 297.

24. *Gleanings*, p. 334.

25. *Gleanings*, p. 8.

26. *Gleanings*, p.8.

27. The two statements quoted may be found cited by 'Abdu'l-Bahá in J. E. Esslemont,

Bahá'u'lláh and the New Era (Wilmette, Ill.: Bahá'í Publishing Trust 1987), p. 170 and *Tablets of Bahá'u'lláh revealed after the Kitáb-i-Aqdas* (Haifa: Bahá'í World Centre, 1982), pp. 22-23.

28. *God Passes By*, pp. 127-57, gives an account of these events.

29. *Gleanings*, pp. 4-5.

30. *Certitude*, p. 98.

31. *Certitude*, p. 99.

32. *Certitude*, pp. 99-100.

33. *Certitude*. pp.103-4.

34. *Gleanings*, p. 59.

35. *Gleanings*, pp. 66-67.

36. *Gleanings*, pp. 65-66.

37. Cited in *Advent of Divine Justice*, p. 79.

38. *Gleanings*, p. 136.

39. *Gleanings*, p. 80.

40. *Gleanings*, p. 164.

41. *Gleanings*, p. 329.

42. For a detailed exposition of this subject see 'Abdu'l-Bahá, *Some Answered Questions* (Wilmette, Ill.: Bahá'í Publishing Trust, 1970), pp. 163-201.

43. Examples, in the words of Jesus, are "Why callest thou me good? There is none good but one, that is, God..." (Matthew 19:17); "I and my Father are one" (John 10:30).

44. *Gleanings*, pp. 177-79.

45. *Gleanings*, pp. 50-55.

46. *Gleanings*, p. 56.

47. *New Testament*, John 1:10.

48. *Gleanings*, pp. 141-42.

49. Shoghi Effendi, *The World Order of Bahá'u'lláh: Selected Letters* (Wilmette, Ill.: Bahá'í Publishing Trust, 1982), p. 117.

50. *Gleanings*, p. 74. In the Bahá'í writings the term "Adam" is used symbolically in two different senses. The one refers to the emergence of the human race, while the other designates the first of the Manifestations of God.

51. *Gleanings*, p. 213.

52. *Gleanings*, p. 151.

53. See Bahá'u'lláh, *The Seven Valleys and The Four Valleys* (Wilmette, Ill.: Bahá'í Publishing Trust, 1986), pp. 6-7; "*Yea, although to the wise it be shameful to seek the Lord of Lords in the dust, yet this betokeneth intense ardor in searching.*"

54. *World Order*, p. 116.

55. *Seven Valleys*, pp. 1-2.

56. *Gleanings*, p. 214.

57. *Gleanings*, p. 286.

58. *Gleanings*, pp. 4-5.

59. *New Testament*, John 10:16.

60. For elaboration on the subject of Bahá'u'lláh's teachings on the process of the maturation of the human race, see *World Order*, pp. 162-63, 202.

61. *Gleanings*, p. 217.

62. *Tablets*, p. 164.

63. *Gleanings*, p. 95.

64. *Tablets*, p. 164.

65. *Gleanings*, pp. 6-7.

66. *Tablets*, pp. 66-67.

67. *Women: Extracts from the Writings of Bahá'u'lláh, 'Abdu'l-Bahá, Shoghi Effendi and the Universal House of Justice,*

(Thornhill, Ontario: Bahá'í Publications Canada), p. 26.

68. A combination of unusual circumstances had made the central authorities in Constantinople especially sympathetic to Bahá'u'lláh, and resistant to pressure from the Persian government. The governor of Baghdad, Namíq Páshá, had written enthusiastically to the capital about both the character and influence of the distinguished Persian exile. Sultán 'Abdu'l-'Aziz found the reports intriguing because, although he was Caliph of Sunni Islam, he considered himself a mystical seeker. Equally important, in another way, was the reaction of his chief minister, 'Alí Páshá. To the latter, who was an accomplished student of Persian language and literature as well as a would-be modernizer of the Turkish administration, Bahá'u'lláh seemed a highly sympathetic figure. It was no doubt this combination of sympathy and interest which led the Ottoman government to invite Bahá'u'lláh to the capital rather than send Him to a more remote center or deliver Him to the Persian authorities, as the latter were urging.

69. For the full text of the report of the Austrian ambassador, Count von Prokesch-Osten, in a letter to the Comte de Gobineau, January 10, 1886, see *Bábí and Bahá'í Religions, pp. 186-87.*

70. *Revelation,* Vol. 2, p. 399.

71. *Tablets,* p. 13.

72. *Gleanings,* pp. 210, 211, 212.

73. *Gleanings,* p. 252.

74. *Gleanings,* p. 252.

75. For a description of these events see *Revelation*, Vol. 3, especially pp. 296, 331.

76. For a description of this experience see *God Passes By*, pp. 180-89.

77. In the 1850s two German religious leaders, Christopher Hoffmann and Georg David Hardegg, collaborated in the development of the "Society of Templers," devoted to creating in the Holy Land a colony or colonies which would prepare the way for Christ, on His return. Leaving Germany on August 6, 1868, the founding group arrived in Haifa on October 30, 1868, two months after Bahá'u'lláh's own arrival.

78. For a description of the disasters which befell European Turkey in the Russo-Turkish War of 1877-78 see Addendum III in *Bahá'u'lláh: King of Glory*, pp. 460-62.

79. *Epistle*, p. 51.

80. Alistair Horne, *The Fall of Paris* (London: Macmillan, 1965), p. 34.

81. Cited in Shoghi Effendi, *The Promised Day Is Come* (Wilmette, Ill.: Bahá'í Publishing Trust, 1980), pp. 32-33.

82. Cited in *Promised Day*, p. 37.

83. Cited in *Promised Day*, p. 35.

84. Cited in Shoghi Effendi, *Citadel of Faith: Messages to America 1947-1957* (Wilmette, Ill.: Bahá'í Publishing Trust, 1980), pp. 18-19.

85. *Epistle*, p. 14.

86. *Certitude*, p. 15.

87. Cited in *Promised Day*, p. 83.

88. Cited in *Promised Day*, p. 81.

89. *Epistle*, p. 99.

90. Cited in *Promised Day*, pp. 110-11.

91. *Gleanings*, p. 200.

92. *Gleanings*, pp. 254-55.

93. *Gleanings*, p. 40.

94. *Gleanings*, p. 215.

95. *Gleanings*, p. 196.

96. *Tablets*, p. 69.

97. *Tablets*, pp. 165-67.

98. *Epistle*, p. 11. The phrase "*Not of Mine own volition*" appears in the same paragraph immediately above the excerpt cited.

99. Bahá'u'lláh's son, Mírzá Mihdí, a youth of twenty-two, died in 1870 in an accidental fall resulting from the conditions in which the family was imprisoned.

100. *Gleanings*, p. 91.

101. *God Passes By*, pp. 94-96.

102. *World Order*, p. 113.

103. *Gleanings*, p. 228.

104. *Tablets*, p. 169.

105. *Epistle*, pp. 11-12.

106. Although Sultán 'Abdu'l-'Aziz' order of banishment was never formally revoked, the responsible political authorities came to regard it as null and void. They, therefore, indicated that Bahá'u'lláh could establish His residence outside the city walls, should He choose to do so.

107. The mansion, which was built by a wealthy Christian Arab merchant of Akka, had been abandoned by him when an outbreak of plague began to spread. The property was first rented and, some years after Bahá'u'lláh's passing, purchased by the Bahá'í community. Bahá'u'lláh's grave is

located in a Shrine in the gardens of Bahjí, and is now the focal point of pilgrimage for the Bahá'í world.

108. For a summary of this body of teaching see *World Order*, pp. 143-57, and Shoghi Effendi's *Principles of Bahá'í Administration* (London: Bahá'í Publishing Trust, 1973), throughout. A fully annotated English translation of the central document in this body of writings, the *Kitáb-i-Aqdas* (*"The Most Holy Book"*), is being published to coincide with the centenary of Bahá'u'lláh's passing, 1992.

109. *Advent of Divine Justice*, p.16.

110. Edward G. Browne, *A Traveller's Narrative* (New York: Bahá'í Publishing Company, 1930), pp. xxxix-xl.

*G*lossary

A

'Abdu'l-Bahá	Eldest son of Bahá'u'lláh.
Abraham	A Manifestation of God who lived in the Middle East about four thousand years ago and who taught the oneness of God.
Adam	Manifestation of God Who inaugurated the previous cycle of revelation – the Adamic Cycle.
Adherents	Supporters.
Adrianople	City in European province of Turkey.
Advocates	Supporters, those who speak in favor of (a religion).
Age of fulfillment	The time when the prophecies of past dispensations would be fulfilled.
·Aggrandizement	The enhancement of power, wealth, position, or reputation.
Akká (Acre)	Prison-city of the Ottoman Empire in Israel.
'Alí Páshá	Prime Minister of the Ottoman Empire during Bahá'u'lláh's exile in Constantinople.
Alienation	Separation from (society).
Allegation	Assertion.
Allegory	Narrative in which symbolic characters and actions express truths or

	generalizations about human existence.
Allusion	Covert, passing, or indirect reference.
Analogy	Similarity.
Animosity	Spirit of enmity.
Aphorism	Short, pithy statement or maxim.
Apostasy	Abandonment of religious faith, vows, principles, or party.
Arcane	Mysterious or secret.
Assimilate	To absorb into the cultural tradition of a group.
Atrophy	Wasting away through undernourishment or lack of use; emaciation.
Authority	Power or right to enforce obedience.

B

Báb, The	Title meaning "Gate" or "Door." The Prophet-Herald of Bahá'u'lláh and the founder of the Bábí religion; the return of the Prophet Elijah, of John the Baptist, and of the Twelfth Imam.
Bábí	Follower of the Báb.
Baghdad	Capital of Iraq.
Bahá'í	Follower of Bahá (Bahá'u'lláh).
Bahá'u'lláh	"The Glory of God," Manifestation of God for this day and this age. Born in Teheran, Persia, November 12, 1817. Died, May 29, 1892.
Banishment	Exile or forced removal from a place or country.
Berlin	Capital city of the German Empire.

73

Bernhardt, Sarah	A famous nineteenth century actress.
Bible	Holy Books of the Jews and Christians.
Blasphemous	Impious, irreverent, or profane talk.
Browne, Edward G.	A professor of Persian at Cambridge University who met Bahá'u'lláh.
Buddha	Title meaning "Enlightened." Refer Gautama Buddha, who founded Buddhism in the fifth century, B.C. He is regarded by Bahá'ís as a Manifestation of God.
Buddhism	The religion founded by Buddha.
Buddhist	Follower of Buddha.

C

Calumny	Malicious misrepresentation; a false charge; a slanderous report.
Certitude	The state of feeling certain or convinced.
Chastisement	Punishment.
Christ, Jesus	Manifestation of God and founder of the Christianity circa 30 A.D.
Christian	Follower of Christ.
Christianity	The religion of Christ.
City of Certitude	The Word of God revealed by the Messengers of God in every dispensation.
City-state	A city that is also an independent state.
Civilization	The process of becoming civilized or developing from a primitive state to a technically advanced and rationally ordered stage of cultural development.

74

Clan	A group of people with a common ancestor, especially while under patriarchal control.
Clergy	The body of persons ordained for priestly or ministerial duties.
Climactic	Of or relating to a culmination or major turning point.
Cohesion	The act or process of sticking together; the molecular attraction by which particles of a body are united; the tendency to remain united.
Constantinople	Founded by the Roman Emperor Constantine, the city was the capital of the Ottoman Empire and is now known as Istanbul.
Corporeal	Having, consisting of, or relating to a material body; not spiritual.
Covenant	The agreement made by each Prophet with his people that they will accept and follow the coming Manifestation of God who will be the reappearance of his reality.

D

Day of God	The dispensation of each Manifestation, esp. the period or universal cycle ushered in by Bahá'u'lláh.
Denunciation	An act of denouncing or condemning.
Destitution	The state of being in such extreme poverty that life is threatened.
Devoid	Entirely free from.

Disarmament	The process of disbanding or reducing a nation's armed forces.
Dispensation	The period of time during which the authority of a Manifestation of God's social or temporal teachings endures. Each dispensation begins with the Manifestation's declaration of his prophetic mission and ends with the declaration of the next Manifestation of God, whose teachings supersede those of the previous dispensation.
Diversity	The state of being different.
Doctrine	A body of instruction – religious, political, scientific.
Dogma	A principle, tenet, or doctrinal system laid down by religious authority; an arrogant declaration of opinion.
Dross	Impurities separated from metals in melting; waste or foreign matter.

E

Ecclesiastical	Of the church or the clergy.
Effusion	The pouring forth of unrestrained expression of words or feelings.
Egress	The act or right of going out or exiting.
Endowment	The act of endowing; the property or talent with which a person or body is endowed.
Equality of the sexes	A basic teaching of Bahá'u'lláh that is one of the prerequisites of world peace.
Erudite	Learned.

Evoke	To call up (spirit from the dead, response, feelings, memories, energies).
Exigencies	Urgent needs or demands.
Exile	Forced removal from one's country.
Exposition	A setting forth, description, or presentation of principal theme(s); explanation; commentary.
Extol	To praise enthusiastically.

F

Fanaticism	A state of excessive enthusiasm and often intense critical devotion.
Focal	Situated or located at, a focus.
Franco-Prussian War	The war between France and the newly emerging Germanic state in 1870 that resulted in the overthrow of the Emperor Napoleon III.

G

Gobineau, Comte de	Famous French historian of the nineteenth century.

H

Heterogeneous	Diverse in character; composed of diverse elements.
Hiatus	A break or gap in a series, account, or chain of proof.
Hinduism	The traditional system of religious beliefs found in India.
Holy Land	Western Palestine (Israel); a land revered by the followers of Abraham, Moses, Jesus Christ,

77

Muḥammad, and
Baháʼuʼlláh.

Holy Spirit The entity that acts as an
intermediary between God
and His Manifestations.
"This link is similar to the
rays of the sun by which
energy is transmitted to the
planets." In order for the
Manifestation to convey to his
followers that he is
animated by the power of
God, he uses symbolic
language concerning the
appearance of the Holy
Spirit to him. Thus Moses
heard the voice of God
through the burning bush,
the dove descended upon
Jesus, Muḥammad saw the
angel Gabriel, and
Baháʼuʼlláh refers to the
Maid of Heaven proclaiming
to him his mission.

I

Ideological Relating to or concerned
with ideas.

Incarceration Imprisonment.

Industrialization The process of industrial
development by use of
machines, especially the
British industrialization of
the eighteenth and
nineteenth centuries.

Iraq A province of the Ottoman
Empire bordering Persia
until W.W.I.

Irony The incongruity between the
actual result of a sequence
of events and the expected
result.

Islam The religion based on the
Qurʼán, which was revealed

| | to humanity through Muḥammad. |
| Islamic Traditions | Collections of stories of the words and deeds of Muḥammad. From these Traditions (Ḥadíth) Muslims model their lives. Shi'ih Islam also includes stories of the Imams, who are regarded as sinless and infallible. |

J

Jesus Christ	See Christ.
Judaism	The religion based on the teachings of Moses.
Justice	Just conduct; fairness; the maintenance or administration of what is just.

K

| Kingdom of Italy | Established in the nineteenth century by the forced integration of the papal and secular states. |
| Kurdistan | Homeland of the Kurds (located in northern Iraq, part of western Iraq, part of south east Turkey, and the northeastern corner of Syria. |

L

Languishing	Growing feeble; losing or lacking vitality; living under enfeebling or depressing conditions.
Latent	Hidden, concealed; existing but not developed or manifest; dormant.
Legacy	A bequest; something material or immaterial handed down by an ancestor or predecessor or received from the past.

Leitmotif	A dominant, recurring theme.
Lintel	A horizontal timber or stone over a door or window.

M Manifestation of God

	The great Prophets of God, his chosen Messengers, who appear in every age. The Manifestations of God are not God descended to earth but are rather perfect reflections of his attributes, just as a mirror reflects the sun but is not the sun itself. All the Manifestations have the same spirit, although their outward forms are different, and they manifest different attributes of God relevant to the needs and circumstances of the age in which they appear. They differ only in the intensity of their revelation and the comparative potency of their light. The Bahá'í writings identify several Manifestations, among them Abraham, Noah, Buddha, Zoroaster, Moses, Christ, Muḥammad, the Báb and Bahá'u'lláh. The Hindu figure of Krishna is also considered a Manifestation, although little is known about him. Bahá'ís believe that there have been other Manifestations but that there is no record of their names.
Massacre	General slaughter, carnage; utter defeat or destruction.
Maturation	The process of becoming mature.

Maturity	The quality or state of being fully developed.
Mazra'ih	The name of the house north of Akká to which Bahá'u'lláh moved from the prison in Akká before taking up residence in Bahjí.
Messenger of God	The great Prophets of God, his chosen Messengers, who appear in each age. They are not God descended to earth but are a perfect reflection of his attributes, just as a mirror reflects the sun but is not the sun itself.
	All the Messengers have the same spirit, although their outward forms are different, and they manifest different attributes of God relevant to the needs and circumstances of the age in which they appear. They differ only in the intensity of their revelation (message) and the comparative potency of their light.
Messianic Expectations	Expectations inspired by the hope for or belief in a Messiah.
Metaphor	A figure of speech in which a word or phrase denoting an object or idea is used in place of another to suggest a likeness between them.
Meticulous	Scrupulous about minute details; very careful, accurate.
Microcosm	A community that is an epitome of a larger unity.
Middle East	The countries of south west Asia and North Africa.
Militate	To have weight or effect.

81

Millennium	A period of one thousand years, especially that of Christ's prophesied reign in person on earth (Rev. 20:1-5); period of good government, great happiness, and prosperity.
Millennialist	Of or relating to the hope or belief in the advent of the reign of the Messiah on earth for one thousand years.
Millerites	A Christian group that eagerly awaited the return of Christ in the 1840s.
Mind	That which in the individual feels, thinks, perceives, wills, and reasons. The mind is the power of the human spirit. For example, the spirit is the lamp; the mind is the light that shines from the lamp.
Mobilization	The state of being prepared for active service.
Monotheistic	Of or relating to the doctrine or belief that there is only one God.
Moses	A Manifestation of God, born in Egypt, about 1250 B.C. who led the people of Israel out of slavery to the Promised Land, and to whom, on Mount Sinai, God gave the Ten Commandments.
Most Great Peace	The period of time when a permanent and enduring peace shall be established. Bahá'ís believe it will be based on a recognition of the character and the acknowledgement of the claims of the faith of Bahá'u'lláh.

Mount Carmel	The mountain in Haifa, Israel, to which Isaiah referred as the "mountain of the Lord."
Muhammad	Prophet-Founder of Islam.
Muslim	Follower of Muhammad.

N

Nation	A community of people composed of one or more nationalities and possessing a more or less defined territory and government.

O

Obligation	A binding agreement; one's duty.
Orient, the	Countries east of the Mediterranean Sea.
Ottoman Empire	Turkish empire ruled by descendants of Osman or Othman I.

P

Palestine	A province of the Ottoman Empire now divided between Israel and its Arab neighbors.
Panorama	An unbroken view of a surrounding region.
Papal States	The central Italian district over which the Pope exercised political control until they were forcibly incorporated into the kingdom of Italy in 1870.
Parable	A short, fictitious story that illustrates a moral attitude or a religious principle.
Paradigm	An example, pattern, or archetype.
Paradox	A tenet contrary to received opinion.

Páshá	Honorary title given to high-ranking Turkish officer.
Patronage	Seeking government jobs on a basis other than merit alone.
Permutations	A major or fundamental change based primarily on the rearrangement of existing electors.
Persia	Iran.
Philanthropies	Active efforts to promote human welfare.
Physician	Healer; doctor or surgeon.
Pilgrim	One who journeys to a sacred place as an act of religious devotion; person regarded as journeying to a future life.
Pogroms	Organized massacres of helpless people.
Pomp	Ostentatious display.
Potency	Powerful, mighty.
Privation	Loss or absence; lack of what is needed for existence.
Process	A natural phenomenon marked by gradual changes that lead toward a particular result; a series of actions or operations conducing to an end.
Promulgate	To make known to the public, disseminate, proclaim.
Prophecies	Inspired utterances of prophets; fortelling of future events.
Prophet	There are two categories: Greater Prophets — independent Prophets or Manifestations, who are the lawgivers and the founders of a new cycle; for example, Moses, Jesus, and Bahá'u'lláh. And Lesser

	Prophets — followers of the Greater Prophets, they are not independent. For example, Solomon, David, and Ezekiel.
Proselytism	The conversion of people from one religion, opinion, or creed to another, especially by the offer of special inducements.

Q

Queen Victoria	Queen of the United Kingdom of Great Britain and Ireland from 1837 until her death in 1901.
Qur'án	Holy Book of Islam revealed to humanity through Prophet Muhammad.

R

Receptacle	A container.
Regress	Movement backward to a more primitive state or condition.
Religious system	System of faith and worship.
Reminiscent	Something so like another so as to be regarded as an unconscious repetition, imitation or survival.
Repercussion	A widespread, indirect, or unforeseen effect of an act, action, or event.
Replicated	Duplicated, repeated.
Resplendent	Shining brilliantly.
Revelation	The laws, teachings, or message of God transmitted through His Manifestations to humankind.
Rome	Capital city of Italy.

S Schism	Division, separation; formal division in or separation from a church or religious body.
Scholar	A learned person.
Sedition	Incitement of resistance to or insurrection of lawful authority.
Sedulously	Diligently; with careful perseverance.
Self-effacement	Placing or keeping oneself in the background.
Seminarian	A student at a school for training candidates for the priesthood, ministry, or rabbinate.
Servitude	Condition of lacking liberty to determine one's course of action or way of life.
Shah	King, especially of Iran.
Shi'ih Islam	One of the two major branches of Islam.
Shiraz	The city of Iran which saw the opening of the Bábí Era with the Declaration of the Báb.
Siyáh-<u>Ch</u>ál	"The Black Pit", the subterranean dungeon in Teheran in which Bahá'u'lláh was imprisoned in 1852 and in which he received the first intimation of his world mission.
Shun	Avoid, keep clear of, eschew.
Slavery	The practice of holding another person as property.
Station	A post or sphere of duty; standing, rank.
Stewardship	The management of affairs as the agent of another.

Subterranean	Existing, occurring, or done under the earth's surface; underground.
Sultan	King, sovereign monarch, esp. of a Muslim state.
Sun of Truth	A title of God.

T

Teheran	Capital city of Persia (Iran).
Templer Movement	German Protestant movement who moved to Mount Carmel in Haifa in the nineteenth century because they believed that Christ was about to return.
Theological Dogmas	Principles, tenets, doctrinal system of religion.
Tolstoy, Leo	A nineteenth century Russian author.
Toynbee, Arnold	A nineteenth century American historian.
Transformation	The act of making or changing form, outward appearance, character, disposition.
Transient	Of short duration; passing quickly into and out of existence.
Tribe	A social group comprising numerous families, clans, or generations.

U

Unification	The process of becoming one; the process of making into a coherent whole.
United Nations	Formed as a result of World War II to maintain the peace and to promote conflict resolution through consultation, rather than force.

| Utterances | Spoken or written words. |

V

| Vouchsafe | To grant as a privilege or special favor. |

W

| Wilhelm I | King of Prussia, 1861-88; German emperor, 1871-88. |
| Word of God | God's message to humanity revealed through each Manifestation of God. |

Z

| Zoroastrianism | The religion founded by the Prophet Zoroaster. |

*I*ndex

89

C

I

96

102